Human Capital: A Guide for Assessing Strategic Training and Development Efforts in the Federal Government (Exposure Draft)

United States Government
Accountability Office

July 2003

HUMAN CAPITAL

A Guide for Assessing Strategic Training and Development Efforts in the Federal Government

G A O
Accountability ★ Integrity ★ Reliability

GAO-03-893G

Preface

One of the most important management challenges facing federal agencies is the need to transform their cultures to help change the way that government does business in the 21st century. Federal agencies must continue to build their fundamental management capabilities in order to effectively address the nation's most pressing priorities and take advantage of emerging opportunities. To accomplish this undertaking, agencies will need to invest resources, including time and money, to ensure that employees have the information, skills, and competencies they need to work effectively in a rapidly changing and complex environment. This includes investments in training and developing employees as part of an agency's overall effort to achieve cost-effective and timely results.

This guide introduces a framework, consisting of a set of principles and key questions that federal agencies can use to ensure that their training and development investments are targeted strategically and are not wasted on efforts that are irrelevant, duplicative, or ineffective. Effective training and development programs are an integral part of a learning environment that can enhance the federal government's ability to attract and retain employees with the skills and competencies needed to achieve results for the benefit of the American people. Training and developing new and current staff to fill new roles and work in different ways will play a crucial part in the federal government's endeavors to meet its transformation challenges. Ways that employees learn and achieve results will also continue to transform how agencies do business and engage employees in further innovation and improvements.

Purpose and Use of This Guide

As part of our ongoing review of agencies' efforts to address their human capital challenges, we saw the need for a framework to serve as a flexible and useful guide in assessing how agencies plan, design, implement, and evaluate effective training and development programs that contribute to improved organizational performance and enhanced employee skills and competencies. This guide was developed in response to that need. The framework outlined in this guide summarizes attributes of effective training and development programs and presents related questions concerning the components of the training and development process. Over time, assessments of training and development programs using this framework can further identify and highlight emerging and best practices, provide opportunities to enhance coordination and increase efficiency, and help develop more credible information on the level of investment and the results achieved across the federal government.

This guide is intended to help managers assess an agency's training and development efforts and make it easier to determine what, where, and how improvements may be implemented. Managers and analysts can use the guide to review an agency's overall training and development efforts as well as training and development associated with a particular agency program or activity. The guide focuses primarily on training and development rather than other important methods of learning within an organization, such as knowledge management. Consequently, users of this guide should keep in mind that this tool is a starting point and that it can and should be modified to fit the unique circumstances and conditions relevant to each agency. Training and development approaches, and how they operate in conjunction with other strategies to improve individual and organizational performance, are continually evolving and changing.

This guide consists of three sections. The first section provides an overview of the four components of the training and development process: (1) planning/front-end analysis, (2) design and development, (3) implementation, and (4) evaluation. The second section of this guide includes key questions to consider when assessing each of the four components of an agency's training and development process, along with elements to look for related to each key question. These key questions ask, for example, how the agency identifies the appropriate level of investment to provide for training and development efforts and prioritizes funding so that the most important training needs are addressed first (planning/front-end analysis). In looking at how agencies assess the extent to which their training and development efforts contributed to improved performance and results, the guide asks about the extent to which the agency systematically plans for and evaluates the effectiveness of its training and development efforts (evaluation). The third section of this guide summarizes our observations on the core characteristics that make a training and development process effective and strategically focused on achieving results. These characteristics include, for example, ensuring stakeholder involvement throughout the process and effectively allocating resources to maximize training investments. A list of related GAO products is also included at the end of this guide.

We developed this guide by consulting with government officials and experts in the private sector, academia, and nonprofit organizations; examining laws and regulations related to training and development in the federal government; and exploring the sizeable body of literature on training and development issues, including previous GAO reports on a range of human capital topics. Major contributors to this guide were Susan

Ragland, K. Scott Derrick, Gerard Burke, and Thomas Davies, Jr. An electronic version of this guide is available on GAO's Web site at www.gao.gov.

We invite comments on this guide. If you have comments or any questions about this guide, please contact me or Susan Ragland, Assistant Director, Strategic Issues, at (202) 512-6806. We can also be reached at stalcupg@gao.gov and raglands@gao.gov.

George Stalcup
Director, Strategic Issues

Contents

Abbreviations

CPE	continuing professional education
GPRA	Government Performance and Results Act of 1993
IDP	individual development plan
ROI	return on investment
SCORM	Sharable Content Object Reference Model

Overview of the Training and Development Process

Strategic human capital management centers on viewing people as assets whose value to an organization can be enhanced through investment. Like many organizations, federal agencies are trying to determine how best to manage their human capital in the face of significant and ongoing change. GAO's model of strategic human capital management[1] identified four cornerstones of serious change management initiatives. These cornerstones represent strategic human capital management challenges that, if not addressed, can undermine agency effectiveness. One of these challenges is for the federal government to successfully acquire, develop, and retain talent. (See fig. 1.) Investing in and enhancing the value of employees through training and development is a crucial part of addressing this challenge.

Figure 1: Cornerstones of GAO's Model of Strategic Human Capital Management

Source: GAO.

Training can be defined as making available to employees planned and coordinated educational programs of instruction in professional, technical, or other fields that are or will be related to the employee's job responsibilities. Training can be accomplished through a variety of approaches, such as classroom training, e-learning, and professional conferences that are educational or instructional in nature. Development is generally considered to include training, structured on-the-job learning experiences, and education. Developmental programs can include experiences such as coaching, mentoring, or rotational assignments. The

---

[1]U.S. General Accounting Office, *A Model of Strategic Human Capital Management*, GAO-02-373SP (Washington, D.C.: Mar. 15, 2002).

essential aim of training and development programs[2] is to assist the agency in achieving its mission and goals by improving individual and, ultimately, organizational performance.[3]

Recent indicators of federal agencies' progress in managing their human capital continue to show that there is significant room for improvement, for example, in agencies' efforts to train and develop workforces with the appropriate skills and competencies to achieve agency goals. Our recent work has highlighted human capital shortfalls, such as insufficient training for employees who lacked needed skills and competencies, duplicative and uncoordinated training efforts within and across agencies, and incomplete information on the extent to which employees had received required training.[4] Additionally, results of the 2002 Federal Human Capital Survey conducted by the Office of Personnel Management showed that only about half of federal employees were satisfied with the training that they receive for their current jobs. As our previous work and these survey results demonstrate, federal agencies face continuing challenges to enhance and improve their training and development efforts. Thoroughly assessing their training and development activities represents a comprehensive first step that federal agencies can take toward identifying opportunities to redirect and intensify their efforts to promote employee learning within their organizations.

Components of the Training and Development Process

Taken as a whole, the training and development process can loosely be segmented into four broad, interrelated components: (1) planning/front-end analysis, (2) design/development, (3) implementation, and (4) evaluation. Figure 2 depicts an overview of this process along with the

---

[2]In this guide, we use "program" to refer to a system of procedures or activities with the purpose of enhancing employees' skills and competencies; we use "efforts" to refer to the consolidated training and development programs of an agency or office.

[3]Training and development in the federal government is governed, generally, by the Government Employees Training Act, as amended, 5 U.S.C. 4101-4120. Regulations are contained in 5 C.F.R. Part 410.

[4]See, for example, the following: U.S. General Accounting Office, *Export Promotion: Government Agencies Should Combine Small Business Export Training Programs*, GAO-01-1023 (Washington, D.C.: Sept. 21, 2001); *Veterans' Benefits: Training for Claims Processors Needs Evaluation*, GAO-01-601 (Washington, D.C.: May 31, 2001); and *Acquisition Reform: GSA and VA Efforts to Improve Training of Their Acquisition Workforces*, GAO/GGD-00-66 (Washington, D.C.: Feb. 18, 2000).

general relationships between the four components that help to produce a strategic approach to federal agencies' training and development efforts. Although we discuss these components separately, it is important to recognize that these components are not mutually exclusive and encompass subcomponents that may blend with one another. Evaluation, for example, should occur throughout the process. For instance, evaluation is an integral part of the planning/front-end analysis as agencies strive to reach agreement up front on how the success of various strategies to improve performance, including training and development efforts, will be assessed. In addition, agencies can build on lessons learned and performance data and feedback from previous experiences.

Figure 2: Four Components of the Training and Development Process

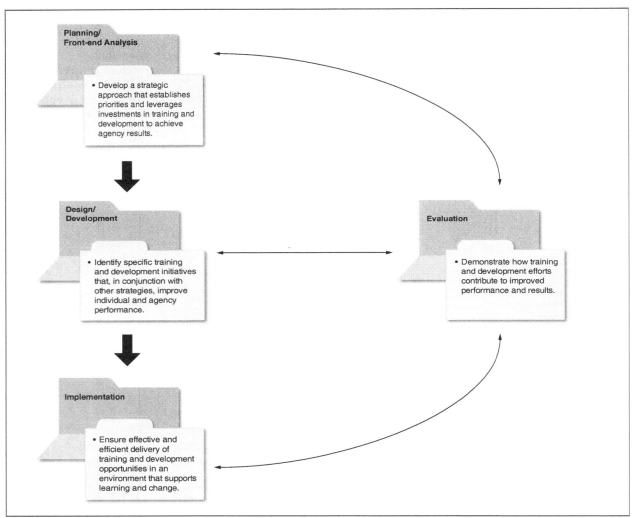

Source: GAO.

Planning/Front-end Analysis

It is essential that agencies ensure training and development efforts are undertaken as an integral part of, and are driven by, their strategic and performance planning processes. Front-end analysis can help ensure that training and development efforts are not initiated in an ad hoc, uncoordinated manner, but rather are strategically focused on improving performance toward the agency's goals and are put forward with the agency's organizational culture firmly in mind. To make certain that their strategic and annual performance planning processes adequately reflect current ideas, policies, and practices in the field, agencies should consider the viewpoints of human capital professionals, agency managers, employees, employee unions, and other critical stakeholders in partnership with agency leadership in addressing training and development efforts. Part of this process must include determining what skills and competencies are needed in order to meet current, emerging, and future transformation challenges and assessing any gaps in current skills and competencies. It is important to note that not all such gaps will be addressed through training and development strategies, or through training and development strategies alone. Rather, strategies involving training and development are but one of the means available to agency leaders to help transform their cultures and operations. At times, for example, training may complement job or process redesign, but in other instances, agencies may identify hiring or other sourcing decisions as the solution.

In addition, agencies should integrate the need for continuous life-long learning and incorporate employees' development goals into their planning processes. Planning allows agencies to establish priorities and determine how training and development investments, along with other human capital strategies, can best be leveraged to improve performance. In addition to planning how training and development strategies are expected to contribute to results, agencies should set forth how the training and development program's contributions to achieving results will be measured. Each agency needs to ensure that it has the flexibility and capability to quickly incorporate strategic and tactical changes into training and development efforts when needed. As the pace of change continues to accelerate, agencies face changes in their missions and goals, as well as changes in how they do business, with whom they work, and the roles that they play in achieving results. Planning and preparing an integrated approach, including training and development efforts, is key to positioning federal agencies to be able to address current problems and meet emerging demands.

Design/Development

Well-designed training and development programs are linked to agency goals and to the organizational, occupational, and individual skills and competencies needed for the agency to perform effectively. Once these skills and competencies are identified, agencies need to determine how a skill or competency gap can best be addressed, whether through a specific training or development program or other interventions. If a training or development strategy is selected, agencies need to consider how the training and development program would work in conjunction with other initiatives to enhance performance, such as changing work processes or providing just-in-time support tools. Regardless of whether agencies use centralized or decentralized approaches (or a combination of both) in managing their training and development programs, agencies need to develop mechanisms that effectively limit unnecessary overlap and duplication of effort and ensure delivery of integrated and consistent messages. As part of an agency's sourcing decisions, it can also help to have clear criteria for determining when to contract for training and development services.

In response to emerging demands and the increasing availability of new technologies, agencies are faced with the challenge of choosing the optimal mix for the specific purpose and situation from a wide range of mechanisms, including classroom and distance learning as well as structured on-the-job experiences, to design training that is as effective and efficient as possible. It is important for agencies to ensure that their training and development efforts are cost effective given the anticipated benefits and to incorporate measures that can be used to demonstrate contributions that training and development programs make to improve results. By incorporating valid measures of effectiveness into the training and development programs they offer, agencies can better ensure that they adequately address training objectives and thereby increase the likelihood that desired changes will occur in the target population's skills, knowledge, abilities, attitudes, or behaviors.

Implementation

Effectively implementing training and development programs provides agencies with the opportunity to empower employees and improve performance. Throughout this process, it is important that top leaders in the agency communicate across the organization that investments in training and development are expected to produce clearly identified results. Similarly, leaders must also be open to feedback from employees. Along with these key executives, the agency's training and performance organization should be held accountable for the maximum performance of the workforce. Likewise, agency managers and employees also have important roles—their input and actions have a critical effect on the success of training and development activities. Managers are responsible not only for reinforcing new competencies, skills, and behaviors but also for removing barriers to help employees implement learned behaviors on the job. Furthermore, if managers understand and support the objectives of training and development efforts, they can provide opportunities for employees to successfully use new skills and competencies and can model the behavior they expect to see in their employees. Employees also need to understand the goals of agencies' training and development efforts and accept responsibility for developing their competencies and careers, as well as for improving their organizations' performance.

In carrying out their training and development efforts, agencies must select employees on a fair and nondiscriminatory basis or provide the opportunity for employees to self-select to participate in training and development programs. Moreover, agencies should avail themselves of the various options in paying for their employees' training and development, and attempt to maximize the use of the training and development flexibilities available to them. Furthermore, encouraging employee buy-in and creating an environment conducive to training and development can go a long way toward contributing to effective learning across the agency. Agency managers should take active roles in setting expectations for learning when they approve employees' requests for training and by reinforcing behaviors when employees attempt to apply lessons learned in the workplace. As with other programs or services that agencies deliver, it is important for agencies to collect performance data during implementation so as to assess the progress that training and development programs are making toward achieving results and to make changes if needed.

Evaluation

It is increasingly important for agencies to be able to evaluate their training and development programs and demonstrate how these efforts help develop employees and improve the agencies' performance. In the past, agencies have primarily focused on activities or processes (such as number of training participants, courses, and hours) and did not collect information on how training and development efforts contributed to improved performance, reduced costs, or a greater capacity to meet new and emerging transformation challenges. Because the evaluation of training and development programs can aid decision makers in managing scarce resources, agencies need to develop evaluation processes that systematically track the cost and delivery of training and development efforts and assess the benefits of these efforts. Providing training is one of many actions an agency can take to improve results, so credible performance data are necessary for considering potential trade-offs and informed decision making. The investment in developing and using measures of efficiency and effectiveness far outweighs the risk of inadequate training. As part of a balanced approach, assessing training and development efforts should consider feedback from customers and employees, as well as organizational results. Agencies can also inform these decisions by comparing their training investments and/or outcomes with those of other agencies or private sector organizations, where appropriate.

Evaluation of an organization's training and development efforts can be complex due to the many factors that affect performance. Agencies' experiences in developing performance measures for other programs, however, are applicable here as well. For example, agencies may identify incremental or intermediate measures to demonstrate that a training or development program is contributing to a goal. It is important to note that the federal government is moving more toward connecting resources with results, and this is no less the case for training and development efforts than for other agency programs. The conduct of evaluations of training and development programs is often discussed in terms of levels. One commonly accepted model consists of five levels of assessment that measure (1) participant reaction to the training program, (2) changes in employee skills, knowledge, or abilities, (3) changes in on-the-job behaviors, (4) the impact of the training on program or organizational results, and (5) a return on investment (ROI) that compares training costs to derived benefits. Some of these methods, such as participant feedback, can help provide better value through continuous improvement. Further, given the large variety of ways to provide training, such as classroom, e-learning, and on-the-job training, agencies need evaluative data to make reasoned decisions about the optimal mix of mechanisms to employ given the specifics of the situation and the objective. The bottom line is that agencies need credible information on how training and development programs affect organizational performance. Decision makers will likely want to compare the performance of these programs with that of other programs, and programs lacking outcome metrics will be unable to demonstrate how they contribute to results.

In determining the mix of approaches selected for evaluations, agencies need to bear in mind the importance of identifying reliable indicators of progress that are aligned with agency outcomes. Training effectiveness must be measured against organizational performance. However, not all training and development programs require, or are suitable for, an ROI analysis. Determining whether training and development programs merit the cost of using such a rigorous approach depends on the programs' significance and cost. Indeed, such evaluations can be challenging to conduct and, because of the difficulty and costs associated with data collection and the complexity in directly linking training and development programs to improved individual and organizational performance, ROI analyses should be done selectively.

Key Questions for Review of Agency Training and Development Efforts

Planning/Front-end Analysis	Design/Development	Implementation	Evaluation

This section contains a discussion of key questions to consider when assessing each of the four components of an agency's training and development process: (1) planning/front-end analysis, (2) design/ development, (3) implementation, and (4) evaluation. Included under each key question is a narrative description along with elements to "look for" that relate to the key question. These "look for" elements should serve as guides for assessment and do not comprise a complete or mandatory "set" of elements needed in response to each question; their relevance will vary depending on each agency's specific circumstances.

Planning/Front-end Analysis	Design/Development	Implementation	Evaluation

Component 1: Planning/Front-end Analysis

Planning/front-end analysis involves developing a strategic approach that establishes priorities and leverages investments in training and development to achieve agency results. Some key questions related to planning/front-end analysis include the following.

a) Does the agency have training goals that are consistent with its overall mission, goals, and culture?

b) To what extent do the agency's strategic and annual performance planning processes incorporate human capital professionals in partnership with agency leadership and other stakeholders in addressing agency priorities, including training and development efforts?

c) How does the agency determine the skills and competencies its workforce needs to achieve current, emerging, and future agency missions and identify gaps, including those that training and development strategies can help address?

d) How does the agency identify the appropriate level of investment to provide for training and development efforts and prioritize funding so that the most important training needs are addressed first?

e) What measures does the agency use in assessing the contributions that training and development efforts make toward individual mastery of learning and achieving agency goals?

f) How does the agency incorporate employees' developmental goals in its planning processes?

g) How does the agency integrate the need for continuous and life-long learning into its planning processes?

h) Does the agency consider governmentwide reforms and other targeted initiatives to improve management and performance when planning its training and development programs?

i) Does the agency have a formal process to ensure that strategic and tactical changes are promptly incorporated in training and development efforts as well as other human capital strategies as needed?

Planning/Front-end Analysis	Design/Development	Implementation	Evaluation

1(a): Does the agency have training goals that are consistent with its overall mission, goals, and culture?

An agency's mission statement explains why the agency exists and what it does. An agency's goals represent the key outcomes that the agency expects to achieve in carrying out that mission. An agency's organizational culture represents the underlying assumptions, beliefs, values, attitudes, and expectations shared by the organization's members. Agencies need to align their activities, core processes, and resources to support outcomes related to these missions, goals, and cultures. In carrying out an agency's mission, senior managers should ensure that training goals and strategies are incorporated into organizational decision making and aligned with organizational goals and culture.

Appropriate accountability mechanisms, such as an active training oversight committee and effective performance management systems, can help to ensure that a sufficient level of attention is paid to planning for training and development needs and that such efforts are consistent with agency mission, goals, and culture. Line managers and supervisors can ensure consistency of training goals with the agency's overall mission and goals by developing their employees with this alignment duly in mind, including approvals of employees' specific training requests. Human capital professionals need to focus on developing, implementing, and continually assessing human capital policies and practices, including those related to training and development, that will help the agency achieve its mission and accomplish its goals. With this level of attention, each agency can better create a coherent and comprehensive framework of human capital policies, programs, and practices specifically designed to steer the agency toward achieving results.

Look for:

- The existence of a training oversight committee or learning board composed of senior and line managers who ensure that training investments align with the agency's strategic goals and organizational culture.

- Evidence that the agency provides training and development for its employees that is aligned with the agency's mission, goals, and culture.

- Analyses of the agency's legislative authorities and policies that may relate to or require training and development.

Planning/Front-end Analysis	Design/Development	Implementation	Evaluation

- An explicit link between the agency's training offerings and curricula and the skills and competencies identified by the agency for mission accomplishment.

- Training and development efforts that target specific performance improvements, such as improved customer service or enhanced public safety.

Planning/Front-end Analysis	Design/Development	Implementation	Evaluation

1(b): To what extent do the agency's strategic and annual performance planning processes incorporate human capital professionals in partnership with agency leadership and other stakeholders in addressing agency priorities, including training and development efforts?

Under the Government Performance and Results Act of 1993 (GPRA), federal agencies are required to prepare strategic plans (updated at least every 3 years) and performance plans (annually) to provide direction for achieving the agency's overall mission. Stakeholder involvement in these planning processes is especially important for federal agencies because they operate in a complex political and legal environment. The involvement of human capital professionals is particularly important to helping the agency in communicating workforce-related goals, priorities, and decisions to managers and staff throughout the agency. To help ensure that agencies integrate their human capital approaches with their strategies for accomplishing organizational missions, the role of human capital staff in the agency should expand beyond providing traditional personnel administration services. Rather than isolating them to provide after-the-fact support, human capital leaders should be included as full members in key agency strategic planning and decision making.[1] This partnership will be particularly important in meeting the newly amended GPRA requirement that human capital approaches be included in agencies' strategic plans as well as their performance plans and reports.

The head of an agency's training and development organization, increasingly referred to as the chief learning officer, has an important role in maximizing the agency's investments in workforce development programs. A training and development organization's responsibilities should include developing training based on strategic initiatives, soliciting input from stakeholders, and prioritizing and scheduling training based on strategic initiatives and stakeholder input. Through early cooperation, the training organization and other stakeholders can work together more effectively because they will better understand how each office or function within the agency contributes to achieving business goals. Concerted and ongoing attention from agency leaders, human capital professionals, and other key stakeholders can directly contribute to the training and

---

[1]U.S. General Accounting Office, *Human Capital: Selected Agency Actions to Integrate Human Capital Approaches to Attain Mission Results*, GAO-03-446 (Washington, D.C.: Apr. 11, 2003).

Planning/Front-end Analysis	Design/Development	Implementation	Evaluation

development of employees who are capable and motivated to accomplish the organization's missions and goals.

Look for:

- Involvement of human capital leaders, as full members of the top management team, in key agency decision making.

- Participation of human capital and training professionals, as consultants to the management team, in the identification of strategies and measures to be used in assessing progress.

- Involvement of the chief learning officer and other human capital professionals in the development and review of strategic and annual performance planning documents.

Planning/Front-end Analysis	Design/Development	Implementation	Evaluation

1(c): How does the agency determine the skills and competencies its workforce needs to achieve current, emerging, and future agency missions and identify gaps, including those that training and development strategies can help address?

Organizations can evaluate the extent to which human capital approaches support the accomplishment of current, emerging, and future strategic goals through the use of workforce planning. At its core, workforce planning focuses on determining the skills and competencies needed in the future workforce to meet the agency's goals; identifying gaps in the agency's current and future skills and competencies; and crafting strategies for acquiring, developing, and retaining people to address these needs. These workforce planning efforts, linked to an agency's strategic goals and objectives, can enable an agency to remain aware of and be prepared for its current, emerging, and future needs as an organization. These needs include the size of the workforce; its deployment across the organization; and the knowledge, skills, and abilities needed for the agency to pursue its current and future mission. To ensure a strategic workforce planning approach, it is important that agencies consider how hiring, training, staff development, performance management, and other human capital strategies can be aligned to eliminate gaps and improve the long-term contribution of critical skills and competencies that have been identified as important for mission success. In some cases, agencies may identify credentials that employees need to perform certain duties, and require that employees meet certification requirements to ensure they possess needed knowledge and skills.

Workforce planning should entail the collection of valid and reliable data on such indicators as distribution of employees' skills and competencies, attrition rates, or projected retirement rates and retirement eligibility by occupation and organizational unit. Agencies can use an organizationwide knowledge and skills inventory[2] and industry benchmarks[3] to help identify current performance problems in their workforces and to plan for future

---

[2]A knowledge and skills inventory is a consolidated list of relevant knowledge, skills, abilities, behaviors, and other competencies that an organization's workforce is thought to possess.

[3]Benchmarking is a management tool used to study another organization's business practices in order to improve the performance of one's own organization. This structured technique generally includes identifying a work activity that needs improvement, identifying another organization that excels in the selected activity, identifying opportunities to improve your own practices, and then implementing these improvements.

Planning/Front-end Analysis	Design/Development	Implementation	Evaluation

training and development efforts that may be needed not only to address performance and skill gaps but to optimize overall performance as well. For example, the movement toward a knowledge-based economy, technological advances, and demographic shifts as the age and diversity of the workforce changes illustrate the importance of investments in training and development for continued growth. Such determinations should include an effort to identify skills and competencies not traditionally associated with specific positions. Failure to make such determinations could hinder individual and organizational performance as the federal government transforms and increasingly uses strategies that can integrate capabilities and provide flexibility to meet new challenges and improve services.

Look for:

- A discussion of workforce planning in the agency's strategic or annual performance plans and reports, or separate workforce planning documents linked to the agency's strategic and program planning.

- Data from agency human resource information systems on such indicators as distribution of employees by pay level, attrition and retirement rates, and ratios of managers to employees.

- A knowledge and skills inventory identifying current skills and competencies of the agency's employees.

- Information on how the agency has identified the roles and core competencies needed to support its goals and service delivery strategies now and in the future.

- Industry benchmarks in such areas as skills, education levels, and geographic and demographic trends.

- Criteria and rationales that the agency uses to determine when to target training and development strategies to fill skill gaps and enhance capacity.

Planning/Front-end Analysis	Design/Development	Implementation	Evaluation

1(d): How does the agency identify the appropriate level of investment to provide for training and development efforts and prioritize funding so that the most important training needs are addressed first?

Adequate planning allows agencies to establish priorities and determine the best ways to leverage investments to improve performance. An agency can aid in this process by developing an annual training plan that targets developmental areas of greatest need and that outlines the most cost-effective training approaches to address those needs. When assessing investment opportunities for its training plan, the agency ought to consider the competing demands confronting the agency, the limited resources available, and how those demands can best be met with available resources. If training is identified as a solution to improve performance, agencies will need to compare various training strategies by weighing their estimated costs and anticipated benefits. This deliberation could include a ranking process using weighted criteria to compare and rank possible training programs. Such criteria could include, for example, expected demand for the investment from internal sources, availability of resources to support the effort, potential for increased revenue, and risk of unfavorable consequences if investments are not made. With this information, an agency then needs to build a business case to support the selected training strategy. Developing a business case for training and development solutions sets forth the expected costs and benefits of the performance improvement investment and provides decision makers with essential information they need to allocate necessary resources. As with any investment, the agency's goal is to maximize value while managing risk.

In addition, agencies should consider succession planning when prioritizing their training efforts. This succession planning includes a review of current and emerging leadership needs in light of strategic and performance planning and identifies sources of executive talent, including those within the agency. Current retirement eligibility trends in the federal government suggest a loss in institutional knowledge, expertise, and leadership continuity, and underscore the need for rigorous succession planning and related leadership development efforts. Agencies also face challenges in the amount of diversity of their executive and managerial ranks, demonstrating the importance of including strategies to address the priorities identified during succession planning as part of agencies' training plans.

Planning/Front-end Analysis	Design/Development	Implementation	Evaluation

Look for:

- Evidence that the agency treats expenditures for training and development not as costs to be minimized but rather as investments that should be managed to maximize value while minimizing risk.

- Goals and expectations for training and development investments that are transparent and clearly defined and whose rationale is consistent across the range of human capital programs at the agency.

- A training plan or other document that presents a business case for proposed training and development investments, including the identified problem or opportunity, the concept for an improved situation or condition, linkages with the agency's strategic objectives, anticipated benefits and projected costs, and ways to mitigate associated risks.

- Evidence that managers provide resources (funds, people, equipment, and time) to support training and development priorities.

- Use of established measures that provide meaningful data on training and development policies and practices and show how specific efforts have promoted mission accomplishment.

- Indications that the agency has identified best practices or benchmarked elements of its training and development programs against high-performance organizations with similar missions.

- Linkages between succession planning efforts and the agency training plan, such as for leadership development programs that are targeted to help address specific challenges related to diversity, leadership capacity, and retention.

Planning/Front-end Analysis	Design/Development	Implementation	Evaluation

1(e): What measures does the agency use in assessing the contributions that training and development efforts make toward individual mastery of learning and achieving agency goals?

In planning the training and development strategies to be implemented, agencies need to establish ways for measuring the contributions that employees' training and development make to achieve results. This process should involve obtaining up-front agreement with key stakeholders on what success is and how it will be measured. In planning future projects and programs, agencies can often learn much from an assessment of performance data and feedback from previous years' experiences. For example, the percentage of an agency's operating budget spent on training, along with other performance information, and comparable industry benchmarks can provide constructive insight into the status of the agency's learning environment. With this type of information, agencies are in a solid position to build on lessons learned and to gain greater insight into the contributions of training and development efforts.

Look for:

- Evidence that the agency considered available performance data and contemplated options for improving future data collection and analysis efforts.

- Assessments of the agency's human resource information system and its capacity to provide relevant and reliable data for fact-based decision making.

- Targets and goals in strategic and performance plans that establish how training and development strategies are expected to contribute to improved organizational and programmatic results.

- Targets and goals in strategic human capital plans to enhance employees' skills and competencies, with measures of resulting changes in these skills and competencies.

- Measures of job satisfaction, productivity measures, and other specific metrics in place.

Planning/Front-end Analysis	Design/Development	Implementation	Evaluation

1(f): How does the agency incorporate employees' developmental goals in its planning processes?

Agencies can use a variety of methods that allow employees to identify their developmental needs and help agencies to incorporate employees' developmental goals in agencies' planning processes. In workforce planning efforts, agencies can survey or interview employees to determine their views and perceptions on training and development in general and more specifically on competencies and skills needed for the future. Employee views can be consolidated with other workforce planning information to identify developmental goals and skill gaps and to assess possible training needs.

Agencies can also identify employee developmental goals through the use of individual development plans (IDP).[4] IDPs can serve as a useful planning tool by providing input to decision makers as they set training priorities and identify future skill and competency needs for the agency. Compiling employees' IDPs using automation can identify these developmental needs for agency managers and can assist the agency's training and development unit in planning and scheduling future courses and developmental programs. IDPs can also serve as a budgetary tool by providing the agency with the opportunity to assess the level of financial resources that might be needed to fulfill employees' development goals. To further assist in planning for financial resources, agencies could also establish individual learning accounts[5] to allocate specific dollar amounts for each employee's training needs. The use of individual learning accounts not only can help agencies in planning needed financial resources for training and development but also will provide employees with an opportunity to assume a greater responsibility for their professional development.

---

[4]An IDP is a written plan, cooperatively prepared by the employee and his or her supervisor, that outlines the steps the employee will take to develop knowledge, skills, and abilities in building on strengths and addressing weaknesses as he or she seeks to improve job performance and pursue career goals. These individual developmental plans are also known as personal development plans, personal training plans, and individual training plans.

[5]An individual learning account is a defined amount of resources, such as money or time, that an agency sets aside for an individual employee to use for his or her learning and development throughout the year.

Planning/Front-end Analysis	Design/Development	Implementation	Evaluation

Look for:

- Surveys of and interviews with agency employees for their views on the agency's support for their developmental needs and particular training and development programs that might be needed.

- Indications that agency leaders systematically consider and act, when appropriate, on employees' suggestions for improving learning products, for developing training programs, and for providing needed resources and useful tools.

- Use of IDPs to identify specific developmental needs and areas for further enrichment for each employee.

- Use of individual learning accounts or other similar approaches to aid the agency's planning and budgeting efforts and to enhance accountability for employees' involvement in their professional development.

Planning/Front-end Analysis	Design/Development	Implementation	Evaluation

1(g): How does the agency integrate the need for continuous and life-long learning into its planning processes?

It is important that agencies treat continuous learning as an investment in success rather than as a cost to be minimized. Agencies may have various reasons for investing in continuous learning for their employees, such as developing the new skills needed for managing change and fostering the skills and modes of behavior needed in flatter, more participatory, customer-focused, results-oriented work environments. In planning training and development efforts, agencies can address employees' career development issues as well as skill-specific training needs. IDPs can serve a useful role in addressing employees' needs for continuous and life-long learning by allowing employees to set short- and long-term developmental goals for themselves. As part of this process, employees should be provided candid and constructive job performance counseling to aid them in enhancing needed competencies.

Whenever possible, the culture of the organization should encourage employees to assume responsibility for their own learning and take an active role in their professional development. In addition, agencies can require employees to complete a specific level of continuing professional education (CPE). Agencies can also highlight the availability of training and development opportunities as an incentive to help recruit and retain employees. Agency leaders must recognize that their organizational cultures can be resistant to change and that they may need to provide incentives for organizational and cultural change and to promote innovation and prudent risk taking.

Look for:

- A statement in the agency's strategic plan or other documents that expresses the organizational value placed on continuous learning and improvement.

- Opportunities for employees and employee organizations to contribute their views on the agency's shared vision and strategies for achieving it, including innovative ideas and process improvements, using ongoing efforts such as input to strategic planning efforts or employee suggestion programs, and fixed routines such as employee exit surveys.

- Feedback from employee surveys, articles in organizational newsletters, Web site links, or other mechanisms that provide information on

Planning/Front-end Analysis	Design/Development	Implementation	Evaluation

employees' perceptions of the organization's learning environment and resulting actions taken.

- Evidence that employee initiatives to build institutional knowledge are valued and encouraged, such as the level of employee participation in professional organizations or the incidence of speaker programs organized by employees to raise their knowledge of key issues.

- Efforts to identify and benchmark with best practices in continuous learning and knowledge management among organizations with comparable missions and service requirements.

- Use of IDPs for both short- and long-term developmental needs of employees.

- Information available to employees about career ladders and how training and development opportunities could help them attain career goals.

Planning/Front-end Analysis	Design/Development	Implementation	Evaluation

1(h): Does the agency consider governmentwide reforms and other targeted initiatives to improve management and performance when planning its training and development programs?

When planning training and development efforts, agencies should look to the actions of the administration, Congress, and internal and external auditors by considering administration priorities, legislative reforms, and major management challenges that might shape agency priorities and strategies for training and development. It is not unreasonable to expect that each new administration may propose different approaches designed to ensure that agencies achieve management and performance improvements and accomplish agency missions and goals. As an administration focuses its efforts on addressing its priorities, agencies can benefit by having mechanisms or processes for considering whether and to what extent these initiatives could be linked to employees' skills and competencies and the related training and development approaches that might be needed. In similar fashion, agencies could benefit from conducting fairly regular and systematic assessments of recent and potential legislative reforms that may affect them. Legislative changes that mandate additional requirements or provide additional flexibility, for example, may affect agency operations and processes in a way that could necessitate new or revised training and development for employees. During planning efforts, agencies should also take into account the major management challenges identified by GAO and applicable inspectors general. These major management challenges—high-profile programs, mission areas, or management functions requiring concerted attention—potentially could be caused in part by lack of needed skills and competencies to carry out the agency's goals. Moreover, these challenges could possibly be addressed in some measure through the implementation of training and development strategies that are linked to performance improvements.

Look for:

- Evidence that the agency is using the administration's metrics (e.g., scorecards) as a method of assessing organizational performance.

- Indications that the agency is systematically assessing the implications of legislative changes on the agency's operations and programs, including its training and development efforts.

Planning/Front-end Analysis	Design/Development	Implementation	Evaluation

- Agency leaders' statements, strategic and performance planning documents, and training programs that are targeted toward addressing management challenges.

- Agency tracking and assessment of its efforts to address the major management challenges identified by GAO and the inspectors general.

Planning/Front-end Analysis	Design/Development	Implementation	Evaluation

1(i): Does the agency have a formal process to ensure that strategic and tactical changes are promptly incorporated in training and development efforts as well as other human capital strategies as needed?

Strategic and tactical changes will quite often influence policies, programs, and practices that have been designed to guide the agency toward achieving its mission. In responding to these changes, senior managers need to continually observe and assess how such changes may affect the agency's human capital strategies and related training needs. A constant watch will help ensure that the agency has a current and valid framework of human capital policies, programs, and practices specifically designed to steer the agency toward achieving its mission. Also, including important agency stakeholders in the process can contribute to an open and continuous exchange of ideas and information. Changes such as new initiatives, technological innovations, workforce attrition, or reorganizations and restructuring will likely require agencies to realign and update the mix of competencies and skills considered necessary, resulting in the need for new or revised training and development programs. Having a formal process for incorporating these strategic and tactical changes will help to ensure that new and revised training and development efforts are quickly brought on line. Capability to adapt to ongoing change should greatly aid agencies in providing training to employees when they need it most.

Look for:

- Periodic reassessments as part of a continual effort to evaluate and improve the agency's human capital systems, including training and development efforts.

- Indications that the agency has communicated and reinforced the relevance of its shared vision among all employees and created, as appropriate, effective strategies for managing change.

- Evidence of timely changes reflected in training and development efforts in response to specific strategies or tactical opportunities and imperatives.

- A variety of training techniques to help employees adjust to organizational and operational changes.

Planning/Front-end Analysis	Design/Development	Implementation	Evaluation

- Plans that describe or outline the way in which the agency intends to incorporate strategic and tactical changes into its training and development efforts, such as contingency plans to address rapid upsurges or declines in demand for training.

Planning/Front-end Analysis	Design/Development	Implementation	Evaluation

Component 2: Design/Development

Design and development involves identifying specific training and development initiatives that the agency will use, along with other strategies, to improve individual and agency performance. Some key questions related to design/development include the following.

a) What steps does the agency take to ensure that training is connected to improving individual and agency performance in achieving specific results?

b) How is the design of the training or development program integrated with other strategies to improve performance and meet emerging demands, such as changing work processes, measuring performance, and providing performance incentives?

c) Does the agency use the most appropriate mix of centralized and decentralized approaches for its training and development programs?

d) What criteria does the agency use in determining whether to design training and development programs in-house or obtain these services from a contractor or other external source?

e) How does the agency compare the merits of different delivery mechanisms (such as classroom or computer-based training) and determine what mix of mechanisms to use to ensure efficient and cost-effective delivery?

f) Does the agency determine a targeted level of improved performance in order to ensure that the cost of a training or development program is appropriate to achieve the anticipated benefit?

g) How well does the agency incorporate measures of effectiveness into courses it designs?

Planning/Front-end Analysis	Design/Development	Implementation	Evaluation

2(a): What steps does the agency take to ensure that training is connected to improving individual and agency performance in achieving specific results?

To help ensure that each training program is connected to improving individual and agency performance, it is especially crucial that agencies analyze their strategic and performance goals to determine where training and development could enhance goal achievement. After identifying the goals that could be enhanced with training solutions, the agency should identify agencywide competencies needed to support these goals. In addition to considering competencies at this "macro" level, the agency should assess skills and competencies for key occupational groups within the agency as well as performance needs and skills and competencies for individual employees. To aid in this endeavor, the agency's training organization can compile employees' IDPs by using a learning management system[6] to identify, prioritize, and schedule training agencywide. A process that enables stakeholders to provide their input, feedback, and ideas into the design of training programs and that incorporates diverse perspectives helps ensure applicability, encourages ownership, and enhances enthusiasm about the programs. Stakeholders should include senior and line managers as well as subject matter, human capital, and technical experts.

Look for:

- A formal training and professional development strategy, or a discussion of training and development in other strategic or human capital planning documents.

- Statements and actions by agency leaders that demonstrate their support and belief in the value of continuous learning.

- Specific steps the agency takes to ensure that employees selected for various positions have the requisite knowledge, skills, and abilities.

- Organizational, occupational, and individual needs assessments, along with causes and reasons for existing gaps as well as possible solutions to those gaps.

---

[6]A learning management system is a software application that helps register, track, and administer courses to a given student population.

Planning/Front-end Analysis	Design/Development	Implementation	Evaluation

- Tracking and other control mechanisms to ensure that all employees receive appropriate training.

Planning/Front-end Analysis	Design/Development	Implementation	Evaluation

2(b): How is the design of the training or development program integrated with other strategies to improve performance and meet emerging demands, such as changing work processes, measuring performance, and providing performance incentives?

When designing training and development programs, agencies need to consider integrating them with other strategies to improve performance and meet emerging demands. Agency managers should keep in mind that a wide variety of interventions can be used to enhance performance and that training alone may not be sufficient and may not always be part of an appropriate solution. In some cases, for example, barriers to performance could relate to insufficient performance incentives or obsolete technology rather than a lack of knowledge or skills. Solutions such as clear and timely feedback on employee performance or a reward system that is properly aligned with employee performance may be key in providing adequate employee feedback or enhanced rewards for improved performance. Other solutions could involve new tools and resources, enhanced technology, or job redesign. It should be noted that although training alone may not be appropriate to correct problems, additional training may be needed to augment changes involving an agency's performance management systems, technologies, or working environment. New ways of accomplishing agency objectives may well require new or revised training initiatives to familiarize employees with these new processes.

Look for:

- Identification of needed performance improvements and consideration of a mix of solutions needed to achieve the improvements.

- Design and use of training and development initiatives intended to complement targeted performance improvement efforts.

- Integrated packages of performance solutions that include training and development initiatives.

- The involvement of line managers, technical experts, human capital professionals, and others needed to develop an integrated way to address specific performance gaps or necessary enhancements.

- Training on building team relationships and new ways of working.

Planning/Front-end Analysis	Design/Development	Implementation	Evaluation

- Cross-training initiatives that broaden employees' perspectives and integrate knowledge about agency operations to improve results.

Planning/Front-end Analysis	Design/Development	Implementation	Evaluation

2(c): Does the agency use the most appropriate mix of centralized and decentralized approaches for its training and development programs?

While recognizing that neither approach fits every situation, agencies need to consciously think about the advantages and disadvantages of using centralized and decentralized approaches, particularly for the design of training and development programs. Centralizing design can enhance consistency of training content and offer potential cost savings. Departments and agencies with centralized approaches may, for example, have established internal "universities" to provide course content to as wide an audience as possible within the departments or agencies. Some agencies have also considered moving toward using learning content management systems[7] as a method of facilitating and centralizing the development of training content using information technology. Likewise, centralization advantages can also continue into delivery and implementation of the programs. Centralization can help agencies realize cost savings through standardization of record keeping and simplified and more accurate reporting on courses, certifications, educational attainment, costs, or standards. A central learning management system, for example, can provide a more efficient means of ensuring quality, administrative efficiency, economy, or adequacy to meet requirements.

A decentralized approach to training design can enable agencies to tailor training programs to better meet local and organizational unit needs. Agencies with decentralized approaches often embed training representatives within their business lines and field structures to assist in coordination of training efforts, including design and development. In addition to enhancing local control over training content, decentralized approaches may enable field offices and organizational units to exert more control over resources and associated costs of training. Overall, some agencies have found success in implementing a combination of both centralized and decentralized approaches by centrally managing reporting and record keeping while allowing some localized management of training content. Whether they use a centralized or decentralized approach (or a combination of both) to design training and development efforts, agencies must limit unnecessary overlap and duplication of effort and ensure delivery of an integrated message when appropriate.

---

[7]A learning content management system is a software application that helps create, store, and manage e-learning content.

Planning/Front-end Analysis	Design/Development	Implementation	Evaluation

Look for:

- Mechanisms to help ensure that economies of scale are achieved by centralizing the design and delivery/purchase of training that has widespread applicability throughout the agency.

- Mechanisms to help ensure that decision-making responsibility is appropriately decentralized for highly customized training needs.

- Unnecessary overlap and duplication of effort in course design and development.

- Inconsistent training content delivered at different field locations.

- Gaps in training provided at certain field locations or within specific offices.

- Uncoordinated purchases of training services that result in higher than necessary overall training costs.

- Different levels or amounts of training provided to groups of employees with similar needs at different locations.

| Planning/Front-end Analysis | Design/Development | Implementation | Evaluation |

2(d): What criteria does the agency use in determining whether to design training and development programs in-house or obtain these services from a contractor or other external source?

Once the agency has identified its training and development needs, it must decide whether to buy or build the solution. Training can be provided by the agency itself, another government agency, a school, a manufacturer, a professional association, or other competent persons or groups in or out of government. To aid in decision making at this juncture, agencies should try to develop clear criteria for determining when to contract for training and development services. Factors that agencies should consider in these decisions include the capability of in-house staff to develop and implement the training; the prior experience, capability, and stability of possible providers in the marketplace; and agency limitations on cost, time, and resources. In certain circumstances, for example, agencies might rely on input from subject matter experts and high performers within the agency to support the design of training and development programs. These internal resources can often provide valuable insight into training design because of their familiarity with the agency's policies, programs, and corporate culture.

Interagency training can be used to supplement the training provided within the agency. Such interagency training can help address common developmental needs governmentwide and promote cost-efficiency by taking advantage of existing resources rather than creating similar programs in multiple agencies. In other cases, agencies might complement the knowledge, skills, and abilities of their staff by seeking outside expertise from consultants, professional associations, and other organizations. Such outside experts could provide cost-efficient and specialized expertise on an as-needed basis, introduce a fresh perspective to addressing the agency's human capital challenges, and ensure confidentiality when obtaining employees' input on related human capital issues.

Look for:

- Efforts to identify cost-effective and robust options on designing training and development programs.

- The explicit use of fair and rational criteria in agency decisions about when and whether to design training and development programs in-house or obtain these services from a contractor or other external source.

Planning/Front-end Analysis	Design/Development	Implementation	Evaluation

- Mechanisms to update decision rules and criteria on an ongoing basis, recognizing changes in such areas as market conditions, agency capabilities, and technological advances.

- Consideration of the consequences of sourcing decisions for the agency, including the impact on working relationships with employee organizations and other stakeholders.

Planning/Front-end Analysis	Design/Development	Implementation	Evaluation

2(e): How does the agency compare the merits of different delivery mechanisms (such as classroom or computer-based training) and determine what mix of mechanisms to use to ensure efficient and cost-effective delivery?

When considering the options of mechanisms for delivering training, agencies need to consider essential issues such as the goals and objectives for the training, the type of audience intended for the training, the nature of the training content, the availability of technology and resources, and the timing for delivering the training. Agencies can use a variety of instructional approaches to achieve learning—in the classroom, through distance learning, or in the workplace. Agencies also need to consider whether to provide individualized instruction or team-based training, for example. When warranted, agencies should consider blended learning that combines different teaching methods (e.g., Web-based and instructor-led) within the same training effort and provide trainees with the flexibilities to choose among different training delivery methods while leveraging resources in the most efficient way possible. When assessing delivery options, agencies can try to achieve economies of scale and avoid duplication of effort by taking advantage of existing course content or training, such as sharable on-line courseware[8] or multiagency training programs.

Many organizations are taking advantage of more flexible design and delivery methods made possible by technology to deliver training to the user's desktop, thereby making training more accessible and cost effective.[9] However, agencies must also consider the technological challenges of various approaches. For example, bandwidth could be insufficient to support desired use of multimedia interactive courseware; concerns about network security may impede learners' ability to access education and training material anytime and anywhere; and technological standards and specifications for emerging approaches might still be evolving. In addition, using distance learning approaches can be a

---

[8]Sharable Content Object Reference Model (SCORM) is an evolving set of technical standards designed to ensure the interoperability, accessibility, and reusability of on-line courseware. Developing Web-based learning content using a standard such as SCORM could allow for easier collaboration across organizations.

[9]Executive Order 13111, "Using Technology to Improve Training Opportunities for Federal Government Employees" (Jan. 12, 1999), encourages agencies to consider how savings achieved through the efficient use of training technology can be reinvested in improved training for their employees.

Planning/Front-end Analysis	Design/Development	Implementation	Evaluation

challenge for some agencies with typical schoolhouse delivery approaches; agency schoolhouses can be resistant to change given that their infrastructure—funding, faculty, and facilities—is often closely tied to student throughput.

Look for:

- A comprehensive mix of formal and on-the-job training opportunities offered to employees.

- A suitable blend of training content that includes both the theoretical basis of the material (such as an explanation of the context and principles involved) as well as practical application issues (such as agency administrative procedures related to the material).

- Decision rules or other information identifying the factors that the agency considers in determining the most effective mix of mechanisms to incorporate into designs for training and development.

- Analysis of cost data on different delivery mechanisms.

- Strategies to continually update training and development opportunities, such as making use of advances in technologies.

- Evidence that the agency is investing in updated technologies and is open to new approaches.

Planning/Front-end Analysis	Design/Development	Implementation	Evaluation

2(f): Does the agency determine a targeted level of improved performance in order to ensure that the cost of a training or development program is appropriate to achieve the anticipated benefit?

An agency's ultimate goal in undertaking training and development efforts should be to optimize employee and organizational performance. In assessing how and to what degree performance could be improved with a specific training program, agencies should try to establish a targeted level of improved performance as well as assess the possible consequences if the training were not to occur. Determining such a targeted level of improved performance can aid agencies in assessing whether the expected costs associated with the proposed training are worth the anticipated benefits. When considering this targeted level of performance, agencies can benefit from considering the implications of both short- and long-term results.

Before committing to provide training, an agency should take into account the potential costs and anticipated benefits of the program. Expected costs of training to consider include development costs, direct implementation costs, indirect implementation costs (i.e., overhead), compensation for participants, and lost productivity or costs of "backfilling" positions during training. Anticipated benefits of training to consider include increased productivity (output), improved quality, reduced errors, and time and resource savings. Such an analysis can help the agency determine whether potential benefits outweigh the expected costs of the training effort.

Look for:

- Specific performance improvement goals in agency planning documents such as performance and strategic human capital plans, workforce plans, and training plans.

- Training and development design and evaluation documents that focus on identifying targeted performance improvements and report on progress in achieving results.

- Identification and consideration of expected costs and anticipated benefits of proposed training and development efforts.

| Planning/Front-end Analysis | Design/Development | Implementation | Evaluation |

2(g): How well does the agency incorporate measures of effectiveness into courses it designs?

The design of a training or development program should involve the formulation of a learning objective,[10] which should be stated in terms that are specific and achievable. To help determine whether such a learning objective will be achieved, agencies should incorporate measures of effectiveness into the courses they design. Defining objectives in a measurable way enables agencies to offer a more convincing quality of feedback. Different types of performance indicators can be used to measure goal attainment, such as input, output, impact, and outcome. Whenever possible, training goals should measure the organizational results being achieved by the training participants rather than be limited to measuring the training inputs or outputs (e.g., number of people trained). Also, performance measures should link directly to the offices responsible for making the programs work. Training programs that are designed to address the agency's strategic goals often do not succeed without cooperation and shared accountability with the program offices.

Look for:

- Clear linkages between specific learning objectives and organizational results.

- Well-written learning objectives that are unambiguous, achievable, and measurable.

- Efforts to ensure that learning objectives have been effectively communicated to all interested parties.

- Procedures to incorporate feedback from line managers, subject matter experts, top leadership, and technical, human capital, and other stakeholders on designing learning objectives and determining which measures are best to determine effectiveness.

---

[10]A learning objective is a statement of the desired changes that the specific training and development program is intended to produce in the target population's skills, knowledge, abilities, or behaviors. Learning objectives are also known by similar names, such as training objectives and instructional objectives.

Planning/Front-end Analysis	Design/Development	Implementation	Evaluation

Planning/Front-end Analysis	Design/Development	Implementation	Evaluation

Component 3: Implementation

Implementation involves ensuring effective and efficient delivery of training and development opportunities in an environment that supports learning and change. Some key questions related to implementation include the following.

a) What steps do agency leaders take to communicate the importance of training and developing employees, and their expectations for training and development programs to achieve results?

b) Is there a training and performance organization that is held accountable, along with the line executives, for the maximum performance of the workforce?

c) Are agency managers responsible for reinforcing new behaviors, providing useful tools, and identifying and removing barriers to help employees implement learned behaviors on the job?

d) How does the agency select employees (or provide the opportunity for employees to self-select) to participate in training and development efforts?

e) What options has the agency considered in paying for employee training and development and adjusting employee work schedules so that employees can participate in these developmental activities?

f) Does the agency take actions to foster an environment conducive to effective training and development?

g) What steps does the agency take to encourage employees to buy in to the goals of training and development efforts, so that they participate fully and apply new knowledge and skills when doing their work?

h) Does the agency collect data during implementation to ensure feedback on its training and development programs?

Planning/Front-end Analysis	Design/Development	Implementation	Evaluation

3(a): What steps do agency leaders take to communicate the importance of training and developing employees, and their expectations for training and development programs to achieve results?

Senior leaders in the agency can play a critical role by clearly communicating throughout the organization that investments in training and development are expected to produce results and that open, candid feedback from employees can enhance the effectiveness of these investments. To better accomplish these efforts, agency leaders should develop a mix of communication strategies to encourage and reward employees for participating in training and development activities. These strategies should focus on ways to foster understanding of the importance, benefits, and expected impact of training and development efforts throughout the agency. Agencies can show their commitment to strategic human capital management by investing in professional development programs that can assist in meeting specific performance needs. These programs can include opportunities for a combination of formal and on-the-job training, leadership development and rotational assignments, periodic formal assessments, action learning[11] and other team-based approaches, and mentoring relationships with senior managers. In helping to develop and carry out these communication strategies, agency senior executives have a central responsibility to foster employee self-development and recognize self-initiated performance improvements, provide training on a nondiscriminatory basis, and establish and make full use of agency facilities for training employees.

Look for:

- Mechanisms for employees and employee organizations to provide feedback on their perceptions and specific experiences with training and development.

- Comprehensive communication strategies to encourage employees to participate in training and development activities.

- Executive-level champions (sponsors) enlisted by the agency to ensure that training strategies are incorporated into organizational decision making and aligned with organizational goals.

---

[11]Under action learning, a group of employees is formed to analyze and resolve an actual problem in the workplace.

| Planning/Front-end Analysis | Design/Development | Implementation | Evaluation |

- Information in plans regarding training and development investments, expectations, and accomplishments.

- Transparent information available to employees though memoranda, announcements, and intranet Web sites related to career maps and paths, competency models, CPEs, and other professional requirements such as licenses and certifications.

- Evidence that agency leaders provide needed tools and resources to line managers and employees.

- Consistent support and appropriate funding for the agency's overall training and development efforts.

| Planning/Front-end Analysis | Design/Development | Implementation | Evaluation |

3(b): Is there a training and performance organization that is held accountable, along with the line executives, for the maximum performance of the workforce?

In addition to the buy-in that occurs through stakeholder involvement in the planning, design, and development of training, agencies need to ensure accountability by holding the training and performance organization accountable, along with line management, for maximum performance of the workforce. The agency's training organization and agency line managers should, for example, make every effort to demonstrate the linkages between the agency's mission and goals and its training and development efforts. These important stakeholders should also work together to establish control mechanisms to ensure that agency employees successfully complete required and assigned training and development. To advance this purpose, agencies must assign authority and delegate responsibility to the proper personnel and establish clear accountability for maximizing workforce performance. Likewise, if agencies expect both their training organizations and line managers to assume greater responsibility and be held accountable for results, agencies must ensure that these key stakeholders have the tools and resources they need to fulfill these expectations.

Look for:

- Evidence that the agency assigns authority and delegates responsibility to the proper personnel and establishes clear accountability for maximizing workforce performance and for achieving the agency's training and development goals.

- Policies, organizational charts, or other representations depicting the linkages between the agency's mission and goals and its training and development organization.

- Indications that training officials and line managers work in partnership to achieve common goals.

- Possible stovepipes in the organization, caused by fragmented lines of communication and accountability, that may contribute to duplicated effort or missed opportunities.

Planning/Front-end Analysis	Design/Development	Implementation	Evaluation

3(c): Are agency managers responsible for reinforcing new behaviors, providing useful tools, and identifying and removing barriers to help employees implement learned behaviors on the job?

To help employees implement learned behaviors on the job, agency managers can work to reinforce new behaviors, provide useful tools, and identify and remove barriers that impede performance. To stress the importance of this responsibility, agency managers should be held accountable for creating an environment that encourages innovation and supports continuous improvement to achieve strategic goals and objectives. Agencies should create the expectation that managers will discuss developmental needs with their employees and identify where training and development is appropriate. Agencies also can track managerial support for training through both enrollment and participation rates in their units.

To reinforce new behaviors, agency managers and supervisors should ensure that their employees understand the importance of using knowledge and skills gained in training to improve performance and are rewarded appropriately for achieving results. Agency managers should also provide useful tools to help their employees implement learned behaviors on the job. Helpful tools such as job aids[12] can minimize or eliminate the need for specific training altogether. Agency managers should also take steps in removing barriers to training and using learned behaviors on the job. For example, managers and supervisors could take steps to address the workday distractions that can interrupt employees' training efforts and actively reinforce the importance of separating "work time" from "training time."

Look for:

- The extent to which managers are evaluated on their efforts to develop their employees and enhance opportunities for employees to improve performance and achieve results.

---

[12]Job aids, also known as performance support tools, are mechanisms for storing information that are readily accessible to the employee and that decrease the need for memorization and thus assist the employee in implementing learned behaviors. A job aid, for example, could be a manual of standard operating procedures, a checklist of key practices, or a computer help system that provides answers to employee questions.

Planning/Front-end Analysis	Design/Development	Implementation	Evaluation

- Responses in employee satisfaction surveys or other feedback on issues related to the organization's culture and working environment.

- Use of feedback from supervisors and participants on the extent to which training and development resulted in changes in individual job performance.

- Policies and procedures to ensure that training and development efforts and expectations are discussed and understood by managers, supervisors, employees, training coordinators, and others.

- Employee feedback on managers' and supervisors' performance in reinforcing new behaviors, providing needed tools, and removing barriers to implementing learned behaviors on the job.

- Examples of tools such as job aids to assist employees in implementing learned behaviors on the job.

- Rewards and incentives for managers and supervisors who consider new ways of working, provide needed tools to employees, and identify and remove barriers to improved performance.

- Rewards and incentives for employees who use new knowledge and skills to achieve results.

Planning/Front-end Analysis	Design/Development	Implementation	Evaluation

3(d): How does the agency select employees (or provide the opportunity for employees to self-select) to participate in training and development efforts?

Agencies sometimes select employees to participate in training and development for a variety of reasons unrelated to the performance needs of the organization or individual.[13] For example, employees have been selected on a sporadic, unplanned basis or as a reward for previous superior performance or contributions. For optimal effect, however, participation of employees in training and development programs should be linked to agreed-upon goals and priorities established by supervisors and their employees. Likewise, these goals and priorities should align with those expressed in the agency's training, performance, or other relevant plans. In addition, employees should be selected for developmental programs based on the suitability and usefulness of the training content. In some cases, employees may already know the material or do not need to know the material to perform their duties.

It is also essential that agencies consider all employees fairly. Agency leaders need to establish procedures to ensure that the selection of employees for training proceeds without regard to political preference, race, color, religion, national origin, sex, marital status, age, or handicapping condition, and with proper regard for employee privacy and constitutional rights as provided by merit system principles.[14] In addition, the agency must follow merit promotion procedures in selecting employees for training designed primarily to prepare trainees for advancement and not directly related to improving performance in their current positions. Because certain developmental assignments can enhance careers and help qualify people for promotion, they should be open to competition, and agencies should advertise these assignments to all eligible candidates.

Look for:

- The selection of employees for training and development opportunities on the basis of agreed-upon goals and priorities.

---

[13]Federal agencies are generally required by statute to provide certain employees with training on computer security, ethics, and management and supervision; in addition, each agency can require additional training for its employees.

[14]See 5 U.S.C. 2301(b)(2) and 5 C.F.R. 410.302(a)(1).

Planning/Front-end Analysis	Design/Development	Implementation	Evaluation

- Selection criteria for executive candidates that are specifically linked to the agency's shared vision and the competencies and broad expectations it has for its leaders.

- The suitability and timeliness of the selection of employees for training and development given employees' current duties and existing skills and competencies.

- Strong indications that the agency recognizes that an inclusive workforce is a competitive advantage for achieving results and that it demonstrates this by working to meet the training and development needs of employees of all backgrounds.

- Actions taken by agency leaders and managers to ensure or enhance diversity in the content and delivery of, and participation in, the agency's training and development programs.

- Procedures to ensure fair selection of employees for training and development opportunities.

- Evidence of union and employee complaints, grievances, or concerns related to unfair or discriminatory training practices.

Planning/Front-end Analysis	Design/Development	Implementation	Evaluation

3(e): What options has the agency considered in paying for employee training and development and adjusting employee work schedules so that employees can participate in these developmental activities?

In general, agencies may pay training and development expenses from appropriated funds or other available funds. Agencies can pay all of the training costs for employees or can agree with the employees to pay some or none of the costs. Agencies also have the flexibility to advance or reimburse employees all or part of the costs of approved training. Expenses of training can include the cost of tuition; purchase or rental of books, materials, and supplies; laboratory and library fees; and travel, per diem, and relocation expenses. In addition, agencies may pay the expenses for employees to obtain professional credentials, including expenses for professional accreditation, state-imposed and professional licenses, and professional certification as well as examinations to obtain such credentials. Agencies can also provide financial incentives, such as retention allowances, to workers who obtain job-related degrees and certifications. Furthermore, agencies have the authority to pay for employees to obtain academic degrees, as long as the training meets agency needs and is not designed only to help an employee obtain a promotion. Likewise, agencies can also pay for employees' student loan repayments.

In addition to the options in paying for employees' training and development, agencies also have flexibilities in scheduling employees' time related to these developmental efforts. Agencies can allow employees to participate in training and development during normal duty hours or during nonduty hours. Agencies may also adjust employees' work schedules to accommodate educational endeavors, as long as it will not unduly interfere with work accomplishment and agencies incur no additional personnel costs.

Look for:

- Evidence that the agency has taken into account the full range of flexibilities in paying for employees' training and development.

- Indications that the agency has considered various options available for scheduling training and development for its employees.

- Oversight systems that ensure employees take advantage of legitimate training and development opportunities and the agency does not pay for fraudulent or inadequate training.

| Planning/Front-end Analysis | Design/Development | Implementation | Evaluation |

3(f): Does the agency take actions to foster an environment conducive to effective training and development?

An environment conducive to training and development can go a long way toward contributing to effective learning across the agency. Agencies can benefit considerably by making use of instructors, facilitators, mentors, and coaches who are engaging, responsive, flexible, knowledgeable, and experienced. This approach, which could itself involve training for trainers and coaches, ensures that these trainers and coaches not only know the subject matter and issues involved but also can effectively transfer these skills and knowledge to others. Agencies also need space, facilities, and equipment that are adequate to meet demand and are favorable to successful learning. For example, employees may need sufficient time away from normal work duties to access computers or simulators to complete a training program. Similarly, agencies need suitable administrative systems that can aid in project management and scheduling of training and development events. Furthermore, proper timing and pacing of training courses and developmental assignments can also contribute to successful learning. This practice can be particularly effective when recognizing the timing that best meets the needs of both the agency and the individual.

The delivery of training and development programs should also recognize specific job processes and procedures in the agency as well as the agency's general organizational culture. It is obviously a waste of resources when training and development programs do not correspond with how specific jobs should be done. To help in this regard, facilitators and instructors should make sure that employees know why they are participating in the training by clearly communicating learning objectives and linking them to managers' expectations and organizational goals. Likewise, because an organization's beliefs and values affect the behavior of its members, the delivery of training and development programs should also take into account the organizational culture of the agency. For example, the culture of an agency that already has computers easily accessible to most employees may more readily adapt to e-learning approaches than that of an agency whose employees have limited access to, or do not rely as much on, technology in carrying out their work. By recognizing and implementing training and development programs that reflect these considerations, agencies can help foster more active participation by employees in training courses and developmental assignments.

Planning/Front-end Analysis	Design/Development	Implementation	Evaluation

Look for:

- Ways the agency ensures that it employs engaging, responsive, flexible, knowledgeable, and experienced instructors, facilitators, mentors, and coaches.

- Evidence that the agency has properly trained managers to coach, evaluate, and conduct employee career discussions.

- Space, facilities, and equipment that meet the developmental needs of participants without creating unplanned excess capacity.

- Administrative systems and databases that enable the agency to properly manage scheduling and support of training and development programs.

- Appropriate timing and pacing for training sessions and developmental assignments given the developmental needs of employees and the mission- and program-related needs of the agency or the federal government overall.

- Efforts to foster active involvement of participants in training and development programs.

- Evidence that the agency's training and development activities appropriately reflect and take into account the organizational culture of the agency.

| Planning/Front-end Analysis | Design/Development | Implementation | Evaluation |

3(g): What steps does the agency take to encourage employees to buy in to the goals of training and development efforts, so that they participate fully and apply new knowledge and skills when doing their work?

Agencies can undertake various steps to encourage employee buy-in to the goals of training and development efforts. Ensuring employee input and ongoing feedback is one important step to increasing buy-in and promoting a shared understanding between managers and employees of training and development goals and related performance measures. As employees develop a shared or common understanding of how their individual and combined efforts contribute to the agency's overall results and successes, they can better focus on their own efforts and priorities. Agencies can use a range of communication methods to build organizational teamwork, including two-way communication between leaders and employees about employees' efforts and their contributions to the agency's outcomes. Agencies can draw on employees' frontline knowledge of work processes and customer needs. They also can empower employees to contribute constructive ideas for improving existing training and development policies and practices as well as identifying additional training and development needs for individual employees and the agency.

Agencies can also encourage buy-in by ensuring employees' ready access to development information, allowing the employees to control their own development and career paths. The availability of opportunities for employees to direct their own learning pace and environment can also enhance employee loyalty. Some organizations have developed comprehensive guidance to help employees manage their career paths and enhance their professional development. Also, some agencies have developed Web-based, single-point-of-entry systems that allow employees located worldwide to access training and career development information. Agencies have also encouraged or required the use of self-directed tools, such as IDPs, to give employees responsibility for assessing their development needs. In some cases, agencies may establish training agreements[15] and continued service agreements[16] with specific employees

---

[15] A training agreement is a written agreement that an agency makes with an employee that provides for promotion or reassignment upon the employee's successful completion of a specific individual training plan within an agreed-upon time frame.

[16] A continued service agreement is a written agreement that an employee makes with the agency to continue to work for the government for a pre-established length of time in exchange for the government's paying for some or all of the associated costs of training.

Planning/Front-end Analysis	Design/Development	Implementation	Evaluation

that allow for employee development while also protecting agency interests.

Look for:

- Evidence that employees are encouraged to identify and take advantage of training and professional development activities and that available training is perceived as relevant and professionally rewarding.

- Indications that agency leaders seek out the views of employees at all levels in developing approaches to training and development and that communication flows up and down the organization.

- Opportunities for employees to work in a learning environment, including (1) access to course catalogs and other training and development events of potential interest (such as conferences and briefings) and (2) availability of self-paced learning when appropriate.

- Policies and use of IDPs and other mechanisms to encourage employee development.

- Rewards and incentives for employees who actively support their own individual development and the development of other employees at the agency.

- Use of training agreements and continued service agreements as career development tools and methods for fully utilizing employees to meet organizational and staffing needs.

Planning/Front-end Analysis	Design/Development	Implementation	Evaluation

3(h): Does the agency collect data during implementation to ensure feedback on its training and development programs?

As with other programs or services that agencies deliver, it is important for agencies to use program performance information in assessing the progress that training and development programs make toward achieving results. Agencies should keep in mind that they need to collect data corresponding to established training objectives throughout the implementation process to refine and continually improve, deliver, and enhance learning. These data include information collected through interviews and surveys, analysis of work samples, and reviews of existing monitoring and reporting data. In addition to information from the training participants themselves, agencies should seek input from trainers, supervisors, coworkers, and customers. Information systems, such as learning management systems and financial management systems, can also provide crucial data for demonstrating results. A rigorous data collection effort will allow for ongoing evaluation of training and development efforts and improve agencies' ability to make needed adjustments.

Look for:

- Information and examples showing how the agency determines when and how to adjust ongoing implementation of training and development efforts based on the agency's tracking of performance data.

- Feedback from key stakeholders on how well training and development programs are working and whether adjustments may be needed.

- Information on how the agency establishes accountability for results of training and development efforts.

- Evidence that the agency collects appropriate performance data during implementation.

Planning/Front-end Analysis	Design/Development	Implementation	Evaluation

Component 4: Evaluation

Evaluation involves assessing the extent to which training and development efforts contribute to improved performance and results. Some key questions related to evaluation include the following.

a) To what extent does the agency systematically plan for and evaluate the effectiveness of its training and development efforts?

b) Does the agency use the appropriate analytical approaches to assess its training and development programs?

c) What performance data (including qualitative and quantitative measures) does the agency use to assess the results achieved through training and development efforts?

d) How does the agency incorporate evaluation feedback into the planning, design, and implementation of its training and development efforts?

e) Does the agency incorporate different perspectives (including those of line managers and staff, customers, and experts in areas such as financial, information, and human capital management) in assessing the impact of training on performance?

f) How does the agency track the cost and delivery of its training and development programs?

g) How does the agency assess the benefits achieved through training and development programs?

h) Does the agency compare its training investments, methods, or outcomes with those of other organizations to identify innovative approaches or lessons learned?

Planning/Front-end Analysis	Design/Development	Implementation	Evaluation

4(a): To what extent does the agency systematically plan for and evaluate the effectiveness of its training and development efforts?

The changing role of government requires not only new organizational structures and innovative ways of working but also an ever-increasing need to assess the best means of fulfilling multiple priorities with limited resources. Agency leaders and other decision makers are increasingly emphasizing the importance of demonstrating results achieved through the significant investments in time and money devoted to training and developing employees. Training and development efforts are often quite complex and challenging to evaluate, however. Since training and development strategies interrelate with other strategies and factors in attempting to change people and organizations, isolating the performance improvements that result from a specific training activity is especially difficult. Perhaps, as a consequence, the traditional approach of collecting and reporting data related to training and development often involved indicators that could be readily quantified, such as the number of employees trained, training hours per employee, and total training hours. While necessary, these kinds of measures do not fully provide agencies with the kind of information they need to determine how training and development efforts contribute to improved performance, reduced costs, or a greater capacity to meet new and emerging transformation challenges.

To measure the real impact of training, agencies need to move beyond these data on inputs and outputs by developing additional indicators that help determine how training and development efforts contribute to the accomplishment of agency goals and objectives. These efforts can be outlined in a data collection and analysis plan, including a description of measures to be used to demonstrate internal influences on productivity and the external influence on customers. Such a plan highlights the importance of having clear goals about what the training or development program is expected to achieve and agreed-upon measures to ascertain progress toward these goals. Developing and using such a plan can guide the agency in a systematic approach to assessing the effectiveness and efficiency of both specific training and development programs and more comprehensively assessing its entire training and development effort. For example, a major program requiring substantial investment merits more focused attention and analysis, so an agency may decide to devote most of its evaluation resources to that program. Planning will allow an informed and strategic perspective for evaluation decisions, however, rather than an ad hoc approach that might result in missing important opportunities and either over investing or under investing in evaluations. Agencies can use

Planning/Front-end Analysis	Design/Development	Implementation	Evaluation

the results of these evaluations for better decision making on whether to modify or redesign training programs or eliminate ineffective programs. They can also use evaluations in decisions about future training and development programs, such as evaluations of data on delivery mechanisms and environmental barriers to improved performance that need to be addressed.

Look for:

- Agency leadership's commitment and belief in the value of training and development as expressed through its receptiveness to and use of results from employees' feedback on developmental needs.

- A data collection and analysis plan that sets priorities for evaluations and systematically covers the methods, timing, and responsibilities for data collection.

- Consideration of various factors, such as the working environment and the job market, that may affect how the agency uses training to improve results, either internally (such as by enhancing productivity) or externally (such as by improving customer service).

- Results of the agency's training and development efforts being widely shared across the organization.

Planning/Front-end Analysis	Design/Development	Implementation	Evaluation

4(b): Does the agency use the appropriate analytical approaches to assess its training and development programs?

When evaluating specific training and development programs, agencies should select the analytical approach that best measures the effect of a program while also considering what is realistic and reasonable given the broader context of the issue and fiscal constraints. In recent years, a growing number of organizations have adopted a balanced, multilevel approach to evaluating their training and development efforts. Such an approach can help provide varied data and perspectives on the effect that training efforts have on the organization. One commonly accepted model consists of five levels of assessment.[17] The first level measures the training participants' reaction to, and satisfaction with, the training program or planned actions to use new or enhanced competencies. The second level measures the extent to which learning has occurred because of the training effort. The third level measures the application of this learning to the work environment through changes in behavior that trainees exhibit on the job because of the training or development program. The fourth level measures the impact of the training program on the agency's program or organizational results. Finally, the fifth level—often referred to as return on investment (ROI)—compares the benefits (quantified in dollars) to the costs of the training and development program.

Not all training and development programs require, or are suitable for, higher levels of evaluation. Indeed, higher levels of evaluation can be challenging to conduct because of the difficulty and costs associated with data collection and the complexity in directly linking training and development programs to improved individual and organizational performance. Figure 3 depicts an example gradation of the extent to which an agency could use the various levels of evaluation to assess its training and development programs. For example, an agency may decide to evaluate participants' reactions for all (100 percent) of its programs, while conducting an ROI analysis for 5 percent of its programs. Factors to consider when deciding the appropriate level of evaluation include estimated costs of the training effort, size of the training audience, management interest, program visibility, and the anticipated "life span" of the effort. Each agency will need to consider the feasibility and cost-

---

[17]Donald L. Kirkpatrick (author of *Evaluating Training Programs: The Four Levels*) conceived a commonly recognized four-level model for evaluating training and development efforts. The fourth level is sometimes split into two levels with the fifth level representing a comparison of costs and benefits quantified in dollars.

Planning/Front-end Analysis	Design/Development	Implementation	Evaluation

effectiveness of conducting these in-depth evaluations, along with
budgetary and staffing circumstances that may limit the agency's ability to
complete such evaluations.

Figure 3: Example Agency's Training and Development Programs Assessed Using Each Level of Evaluation

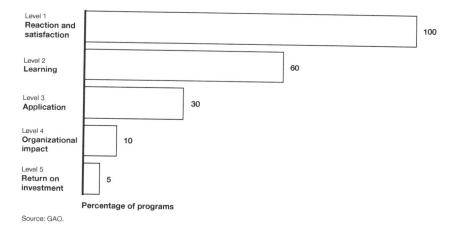

Level 1
Reaction and satisfaction — 100

Level 2
Learning — 60

Level 3
Application — 30

Level 4
Organizational impact — 10

Level 5
Return on investment — 5

Percentage of programs

Source: GAO.

Look for:

- Demonstrated efforts to use appropriate methods to evaluate training and development efforts that recognize the feasibility and cost-effectiveness of specific evaluation efforts.

- Guidelines or criteria for determining when and how the agency's training programs will be evaluated using different levels or analytical methods.

- Measures of training participants' reaction to, and satisfaction with, the training program or planned actions to use new or enhanced competencies.

- Measures of changes in knowledge, skills, and abilities; on-the-job behavior and progress on planned actions; and organizational impact.

Planning/Front-end Analysis	Design/Development	Implementation	Evaluation

- Comparisons of benefits (including qualitative, estimated, and in some cases monetized benefits) to the costs of the training and development program.

Planning/Front-end Analysis	Design/Development	Implementation	Evaluation

4(c): What performance data (including qualitative and quantitative measures) does the agency use to assess the results achieved through training and development efforts?

Successful organizations typically develop and implement human capital approaches based on a thorough assessment of the organizations' specific needs and capabilities. Valid and reliable data are the starting point for such assessments. To assess the results achieved through training and development, agencies can rely upon hard (quantitative) data, such as productivity/output, quality, costs, and time, or soft (qualitative) data, such as feedback on how well a training program satisfied employees' expectations. By taking steps to agree on measures of success up front, agency officials can decide on the objectives for each training and development program. For example, for an agency that has designed and implemented a program to train its employees on new procedures for processing specific applications, measures of productivity (output) could involve the number of applications processed per day, quality could be the number of errors per 1,000 applications processed, time could be the average number of hours to process each application, and cost could involve the total cost to process each application. Soft data could include employees' and managers' views, collected through questionnaires, on the extent to which employees applied the content of the training program to their jobs. For employees whose work is not as quantifiable, it is even more important that agency officials agree up front on the training program's objectives and how performance toward these objectives is to be evaluated. By engaging a broad perspective, agencies can help ensure buy-in from stakeholders about how training and development programs are assessed. These perspectives can also contribute to agencies' efforts to ensure that the data they use are verified and reliable. Logic models,[18] the use of intermediate measures, and other approaches can help decision makers understand linkages, especially for developmental programs, where outcomes may not be apparent for several years.

As part of a balanced approach, assessing training and development efforts should also consider feedback from customers, such as whether employee behaviors or agency processes and services effectively met their needs and expectations. Using a balanced approach that reflects feedback from

---

[18]A logic model is an evaluation tool used to describe a program's components and desired results and explain the strategy—or logic—by which the program is expected to achieve its goals. By specifying what is expected at each step, a logic model can help define measures of the program's progress towards its ultimate goals.

Planning/Front-end Analysis	Design/Development	Implementation	Evaluation

customers and employees, as well as organizational results, is particularly important as agencies transform their cultures and operations. In addition, because the work of federal employees can be complex and often cannot be reduced to a single task, a balanced approach to both the types and sources of data helps to strengthen the linkages between training and development programs and improved performance.

Look for:

- Use of both quantitative and qualitative measures to assess training results, in areas such as increased productivity and improved job satisfaction.

- Use of a balanced set of measures that reflect feedback from employees and customers and organizational results.

- Use of measurement tools, such as templates, that assist in systematically collecting valid and reliable performance data.

- Determined efforts to improve the quality of performance data.

Planning/Front-end Analysis	Design/Development	Implementation	Evaluation

4(d): How does the agency incorporate evaluation feedback into the planning, design, and implementation of its training and development efforts?

An agency should view its training and development efforts not as a static, after-the-fact requirement but as a continual, ongoing effort throughout the planning, design, and implementation components of the process. When undertaking planning and front-end analysis, the agency should make a concerted effort to identify and use focused and relevant data and measures that will aid in guiding future training and development efforts. These considerations may highlight the need for the agency to reassess what types of data it currently collects, how such data might be improved for future assessments, and how to build in agreed-upon measures up front to continually measure results.

For design and development of training, agencies should rely on evaluations and benchmarking to determine what approaches work best given all the related elements, such as the proposed audience for the training program, the material to be covered, and possible delivery mechanisms that could be employed. Building in such evaluation feedback will help to identify and remove obstacles to successful implementation. Reviewing staff and instructor feedback regularly is also important to improving the overall process and thus increasing the likelihood of success. Catching potential problems at the early stages of the process can save valuable time and resources that a major redesign of training would likely entail. Agencies can use evaluation feedback to identify problems and improve training and development programs as needed, either by making incremental changes or redesigning the entire training effort to incorporate major changes.

Look for:

- Indications that the agency is making fact-based determinations of the impact of its training and development programs by using these assessments to refine or redesign training and development efforts as needed.

- Systematic monitoring and feedback processes.

- Informal feedback mechanisms.

Planning/Front-end Analysis	Design/Development	Implementation	Evaluation

- Information showing that the agency reallocates or redirects its resources based on data derived from evaluating its training and development activities.

- Examples of evaluations, and possible resulting changes made, during the planning/front-end analysis, design/development, and implementation components of the training and development process.

- Indications of a program for bestowing awards, recognition, and incentives on the basis of meeting or exceeding targets related to improving training and development.

Planning/Front-end Analysis	Design/Development	Implementation	Evaluation

4(e): Does the agency incorporate different perspectives (including those of line managers and staff, customers, and experts in areas such as financial, information, and human capital management) in assessing the impact of training on performance?

To the extent possible, agencies need to ensure that they incorporate a wide variety of stakeholder perspectives in assessing the impact of training on employee and agency performance. Stakeholders' perspectives can be obtained through surveys and questionnaires, individual or group interviews, or communication with more formal multidisciplinary bodies such as advisory or education councils. The sources of such information could include the training participants themselves; training designers, developers, and facilitators; agency leaders, managers, supervisors, subordinates, and coworkers; employee organizations; internal and external customers; and functional and subject matter experts. To complete valid and useful evaluations, it could be helpful to address the possibility of low participation on the part of employees and managers in surveys and focus groups that may limit that agency's access to these important data.

Situations in which stakeholders could offer their perspectives abound. Training participants can provide valuable information on whether they were satisfied with the training, learned from the effort, and used these new skills and competencies on their jobs to improve results. Training facilitators can provide useful perspectives by observing the extent to which trainees are absorbing the training material and demonstrating newly acquired skills in the training environment. Managers, supervisors, subordinates, and coworkers can often provide practical insight on the extent to which employees' on-the-job behavior changed in light of training and development efforts. Internal and external customers can also provide worthwhile feedback to agencies about the extent to which employee performance has improved, particularly for competencies related to customer service. Lastly, subject matter experts and functional specialists may use feedback from trainees and instructors as the basis for their own valuable insights regarding the appropriate level of detail provided in a particular training program. Such insights play an important role in helping agencies find a comfortable median between overly broad and unduly detailed course content.

Planning/Front-end Analysis	Design/Development	Implementation	Evaluation

Look for:

- Surveys and questionnaires of stakeholders, such as employees, supervisors, managers, customers, subject matter experts, and advisory councils.

- Interviews and focus group meetings with stakeholders.

- Responsive and timely efforts to collect and analyze individuals' perspectives and to use this feedback to improve or redesign training programs when necessary.

Planning/Front-end Analysis	Design/Development	Implementation	Evaluation

4(f): How does the agency track the cost and delivery of its training and development programs?

Agency managers and supervisors are often aware that investments—both monetary and nonmonetary—in training and development initiatives can be quite large. However, across the federal government, evaluation efforts have often been hindered by the lack of accurate and reliable data to document the total costs of training efforts. To obtain a comprehensive determination of the costs of these initiatives, agencies need to find ways around barriers that prevent them from fully and accurately identifying the expenses associated with all components of their training and development processes. These costs can include expenses for instructional development; participant and instructor attendance; facility, material, and equipment costs; as well as travel and per diem expenses. To track the cost and delivery of training and development programs, agencies need credible and reliable data from learning management systems as well as accounting, financial, and performance reporting systems. To the extent possible, agencies also need to ensure data consistency across the organization. Variation in the methods used to collect data can greatly affect the analysis of uniform, quality data on the cost and delivery of training and development programs.

Look for:

- A comprehensive learning management system that can track the delivery of training within the agency.

- Accounting, financial, and performance reporting systems that produce credible, reliable, and consistent data on agency activities, including training and development programs.

- Identification and tracking of the associated costs of specific training and development programs.

- Concerted efforts to ensure the quality of agency data, such as improving administrative data systems as an aid to more relevant and reliable data and possibly conducting special data collections when necessary.

- Barriers to providing a comprehensive picture of costs, expenses, and other financial information related to training and development activities.

Planning/Front-end Analysis	Design/Development	Implementation	Evaluation

4(g): How does the agency assess the benefits achieved through training and development programs?

In addition to isolating and tracking the costs associated with training and development programs, agencies should also endeavor to identify the associated benefits of such efforts. These benefits can include, for example, increased productivity, enhanced customer satisfaction, increased quality, reduced errors, or decreased costs. From an agency's perspective, the benefits derived from a specific training and development program are of greatest significance when employees directly apply newly acquired learning in their individual job performance and, ultimately, their collective performance. Employee surveys or exit interviews may provide information on whether the agency's training and development programs help or hinder recruitment or retention, as access to training and a learning environment are important factors for some individuals.

An agency can use various analytical methods in attempting to assess the impact of a training and development program on individual and organizational performance. Feedback from stakeholders can provide estimates on the degree to which they believe improvement can be attributed to training. Using specific measures, agencies can also use performance tracking to monitor the performance of individuals and work units after training is completed to obtain before-and-after comparisons of performance. The use of control groups is another method agencies could consider to help reveal differences between the job performance of trained and untrained employees. Forward-looking approaches such as trend analysis and forecasting can serve as ways to estimate future performance without the training, thus allowing for a comparison with post-training performance. When using any of these analytical methods, agencies should keep in mind that the lack of change in employees' behavior after training does not necessarily mean that the training program was ineffective. Other factors such as incentives and work environment can also influence employees' use of newly acquired skills and competencies on their jobs.

The agency may decide it should take steps to determine whether the benefits derived from the training and development program are worth the associated costs. One way of looking at this is calculating how long it will take before the benefits from the training outweigh the projected costs. This information would be useful, for example, in establishing priorities among training and development programs, as well as in comparing training or development programs with other potential strategies and

Planning/Front-end Analysis	Design/Development	Implementation	Evaluation

determining how effectively they could work together to improve performance.

Once benefits are identified, the agency can then decide whether to attempt to convert these benefits into a monetary value to calculate an ROI. Estimating the monetary value of these benefits is one of the most challenging parts of the effort to determine the ROI for a given training and development program. Converting some benefits into dollar amounts is straightforward, but other associated benefits may be much more difficult to translate into dollars. Once these costs and benefits have been estimated, the agency can then calculate an ROI ratio for the training program. In some cases, such as those involving initial e-learning experiences, agencies may be able to identify immediate cost savings through reduced time, travel, and facility costs—and there may be sizeable investment start-up costs for e-learning as well. The key point remains— agencies' evaluations must be able to demonstrate that employees are learning and retaining the information provided in training or development programs. For example, e-learning may be more effective in some instances, while in others the topics or the employees may not learn as well from e-learning as through other methods. The bottom line is the extent to which any training and development program engages participants and helps improve employee and organizational performance.

Look for:

- Use of control groups to reveal possible differences between trained and untrained employees.

- Stakeholder feedback and estimates on improvements attributed to a training and development program.

- Use of forward-looking analytical approaches, such as forecasting and trend analysis, to aid in estimating and comparing future performance with and without the training intervention.

- Conversions of identified training benefits to monetary values.

- Comparisons of the associated costs and monetized benefits of training programs to determine an ROI.

Planning/Front-end Analysis	Design/Development	Implementation	Evaluation

- Use of data on associated benefits and the results of ROI analyses in the agency's decision making processes for refining, redesigning, or terminating specific training and development programs.

Planning/Front-end Analysis	Design/Development	Implementation	Evaluation

4(h): Does the agency compare its training investments, methods, or outcomes with those of other organizations to identify innovative approaches or lessons learned?

To aid in the effort of using data-driven assessments to develop and implement human capital approaches, agencies can compare their training investments, methods, or outcomes with those of other organizations. There are many ways to help improve performance, so it is important for agencies to continually look to others to identify innovative approaches that may relate to their training and development efforts. For example, strategies such as blended learning can offer various options to provide needed interactions, participant feedback, and access to experts. Information on how leading organizations use e-learning can provide valuable input as agencies enhance their capabilities. Job aids, and other strategies to provide performance support embedded in the workflow, will also continue to affect when and how easily employees can obtain the information and skills they need to do their work, which shapes how the agency can best use its training and development investments.

Benchmarking is a technique that can help agencies determine who is the very best, who sets the standard, and what that standard is. With these data in hand, an agency can use benchmarking to compare its investments, approaches, and outcomes with those of public and private organizations that are undertaking notably innovative and effective training and development efforts. Of course, this must be done within the context of that agency's unique environment and situation. Organizations can successfully use benchmarking to increase productivity and quality through an understanding of what level of performance is possible and why a gap exists between current and optimal performance. Using these benchmarks, agencies can uncover weaknesses in their training and development strategies that need improvement and identify new ideas, mechanisms, and metrics that they could employ. As is often the case, agencies informed by such benchmarking of effective practices are likely to develop their own innovative approaches and lessons learned for improving individual and organizational performance.

Look for:

- Concerted efforts to identify agency work practices related to training and development that need improvement.

- Attempts to identify innovative and effective training and development efforts outside of the agency for possible benchmarking.

Planning/Front-end Analysis	Design/Development	Implementation	Evaluation

- Comparisons of the agency's activities and processes with those of other organizations considered "best in class" for particular training and development efforts.

- Implementation of identified benchmark solutions to improve performance.

Summary Observations on the Training and Development Process

Our examination of major issues to consider when assessing an agency's training and development efforts revealed certain core characteristics that constitute a strategic training and development process. We identified these core characteristics by analyzing and categorizing the various "look for" elements associated with the key questions, as described in section 2 of this guide. Figure 4 lists and summarizes the eight core characteristics of the training and development process that we identified as part of preparing this guide. We believe that a concerted effort to integrate these core characteristics can further each agency's efforts to continually improve its training and development process. Conversely, identifying where an agency's training and development process lacks these core characteristics can help address barriers that hinder its ability to achieve meaningful results.

Figure 4: Core Characteristics of a Strategic Training and Development Process

- **Strategic alignment.** Clear linkages exist between the agency's mission, goals, and culture and its training and development efforts. The agency's mission and goals drive a strategic training and development approach and help ensure that the agency takes full advantage of an optimal mix of strategies to improve performance and enhance capacity to meet new and emerging challenges.

- **Leadership commitment and communication.** Agency leaders and managers consistently demonstrate that they support and value continuous learning, are receptive to and use feedback from employees on developmental needs and training results, and set the expectation that fair and effective training and development practices will improve individual and organizational performance.

- **Stakeholder involvement.** Agency stakeholders are involved throughout the training and development process to help ensure that different perspectives are taken into account and contribute to effective training and development programs. Stakeholders' views are incorporated in identifying needed performance enhancements, developing and effectively implementing well-thought-out strategies, and helping to conceptualize and use balanced measures that accurately reflect the extent to which training and development efforts contribute toward achieving results.

- **Accountability and recognition.** Appropriate accountability mechanisms, such as performance management systems, are in place to hold managers and employees responsible for learning and working in new ways. Appropriate rewards and incentives exist and are used fairly and equitably to encourage innovation, reinforce changed behaviors, and enhance performance.

- **Effective resource allocation.** The agency provides an appropriate level of funding and other tools and resources—along with external expertise and assistance when needed—to ensure that its training and development programs reflect the importance of its investment in human capital to achieving its mission and goals.

- **Partnerships and learning from others.** Coordination within and among agencies achieves economies of scale and limits duplication of efforts. In addition to benchmarking high-performing organizations, these efforts allow an agency to keep abreast of current practices, enhance efficiency, and increase the effectiveness of its training and development programs.

- **Data quality assurance.** The agency has established policies and procedures that recognize and support the importance of quality data and of evaluating the quality and effectiveness of training and development efforts. It establishes valid measures and validated systems to provide reliable and relevant information that is useful in improving the agency's training and development efforts.

- **Continuous performance improvement.** Agency practices and policies foster a culture of continuous improvement and optimal organizational performance regarding training and other activities. Stakeholders rely on and use program performance information and other data to assess and refine ongoing training and development efforts; target new initiatives to improve performance; and design, develop, and implement new approaches to train and develop employees.

Source: GAO.

When using this guide to assess an agency's training and development efforts, it is important to recognize how these eight core characteristics can contribute to a strategic training and development approach. Each

characteristic, such as stakeholder involvement, is a crucial part of each
component and should be integrated throughout the training and
development process. (See fig. 5.)

**Figure 5: Linking Core Characteristics to the Components of the Training and
Development Process**

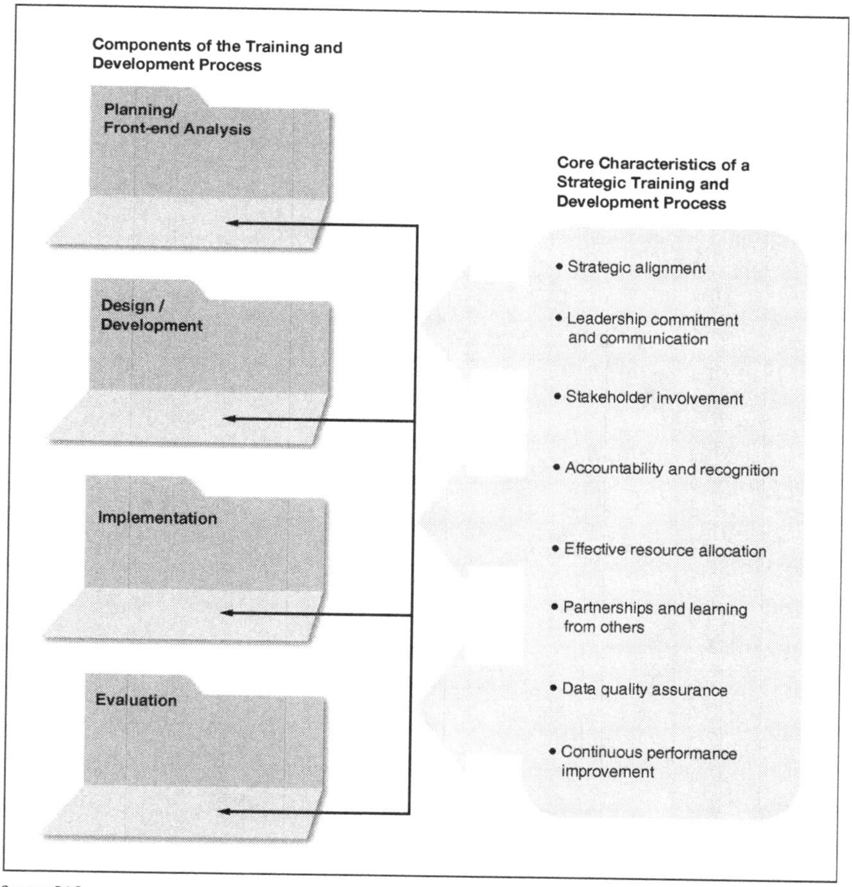

Source: GAO.

For example, in planning/front-end analysis, all of an agency's
stakeholders, including human capital and training professionals, should

be involved in decisions about how best to achieve strategic and performance goals through targeted training and development strategies. When designing and developing a specific training or development program, subject matter experts can contribute their knowledge and perspectives about what is needed to master the job's requirements and help identify which performance measures would best gauge the effectiveness of the training or development program. In implementation, trainers and participants can provide valuable feedback on how training efforts are going and point to refinements or additions that may be needed. Evaluation can be informed, not only through participants' reactions, but also through involving stakeholders such as peers, managers, or others who are in a position to observe behavioral or organizational changes and provide information on how training and development efforts contributed to these changes.

Related GAO Products

Human Capital: Selected Agency Actions to Integrate Human Capital Approaches to Attain Mission Results. GAO-03-446. Washington, D.C.: April 11, 2003.

Military Transformation: Progress and Challenges for DOD's Advanced Distributed Learning Programs. GAO-03-393. Washington, D.C.: February 28, 2003.

Defense Management: Army Needs to Address Resource and Mission Requirements Affecting Its Training and Doctrine Command. GAO-03-214. Washington, D.C.: February 10, 2003.

Information Technology Training: Practices of Leading Private-Sector Companies. GAO-03-390. Washington, D.C.: January 31, 2003.

Human Capital: Effective Use of Flexibilities Can Assist Agencies in Managing Their Workforces. GAO-03-2. Washington, D.C.: December 6, 2002.

A Model of Strategic Human Capital Management. GAO-02-373SP. Washington, D.C.: March 15, 2002.

Export Promotion: Government Agencies Should Combine Small Business Export Training Programs. GAO-01-1023. Washington, D.C.: September 21, 2001.

Human Capital: Practices That Empowered and Involved Employees. GAO-01-1070. Washington, D.C.: September 14, 2001.

Veterans' Benefits: Training for Claims Processors Needs Evaluation. GAO-01-601. Washington, D.C.: May 31, 2001.

Human Capital: A Self-Assessment Checklist for Agency Leaders. GAO/OCG-00-14G. Washington, D.C.: September 1, 2000.

Human Capital: Design, Implementation, and Evaluation of Training at Selected Agencies. GAO/T-GGD-00-131. Washington, D.C.: May 18, 2000.

Acquisition Reform: GSA and VA Efforts to Improve Training of Their Acquisition Workforces. GAO/GGD-00-66. Washington, D.C.: February 18, 2000.

Human Capital: Key Principles From Nine Private Sector Organizations. GAO/GGD-00-28. Washington, D.C.: January 31, 2000.

Department of Energy: Actions Necessary to Improve DOE's Training Program. GAO/RCED-99-56. Washington, D.C.: February 12, 1999.

GAO's Mission	The General Accounting Office, the audit, evaluation and investigative arm of Congress, exists to support Congress in meeting its constitutional responsibilities and to help improve the performance and accountability of the federal government for the American people. GAO examines the use of public funds; evaluates federal programs and policies; and provides analyses, recommendations, and other assistance to help Congress make informed oversight, policy, and funding decisions. GAO's commitment to good government is reflected in its core values of accountability, integrity, and reliability.

Obtaining Copies of GAO Reports and Testimony	The fastest and easiest way to obtain copies of GAO documents at no cost is through the Internet. GAO's Web site (www.gao.gov) contains abstracts and full-text files of current reports and testimony and an expanding archive of older products. The Web site features a search engine to help you locate documents using key words and phrases. You can print these documents in their entirety, including charts and other graphics. Each day, GAO issues a list of newly released reports, testimony, and correspondence. GAO posts this list, known as "Today's Reports," on its Web site daily. The list contains links to the full-text document files. To have GAO e-mail this list to you every afternoon, go to www.gao.gov and select "Subscribe to e-mail alerts" under the "Order GAO Products" heading.

Order by Mail or Phone	The first copy of each printed report is free. Additional copies are $2 each. A check or money order should be made out to the Superintendent of Documents. GAO also accepts VISA and Mastercard. Orders for 100 or more copies mailed to a single address are discounted 25 percent. Orders should be sent to: U.S. General Accounting Office 441 G Street NW, Room LM Washington, D.C. 20548 To order by Phone: Voice: (202) 512-6000 TDD: (202) 512-2537 Fax: (202) 512-6061

To Report Fraud, Waste, and Abuse in Federal Programs	Contact: Web site: www.gao.gov/fraudnet/fraudnet.htm E-mail: fraudnet@gao.gov Automated answering system: (800) 424-5454 or (202) 512-7470

Public Affairs	Jeff Nelligan, Managing Director, NelliganJ@gao.gov (202) 512-4800 U.S. General Accounting Office, 441 G Street NW, Room 7149 Washington, D.C. 20548

PRINTED ON RECYCLED PAPER

United States
General Accounting Office
Washington, D.C. 20548-0001

Official Business
Penalty for Private Use $300

Address Service Requested

9 781240 685547